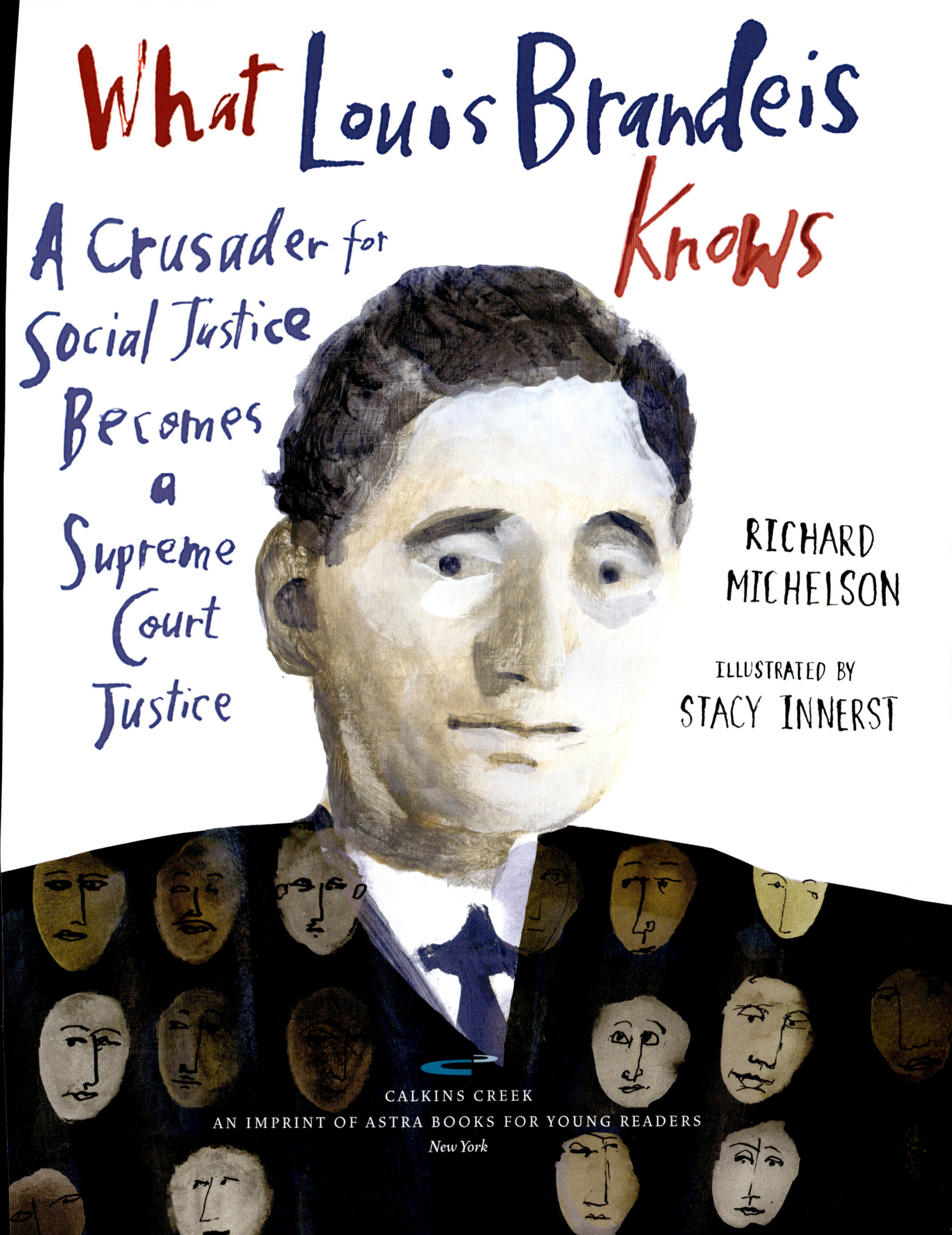

What Louis Brandeis Knows

A Crusader for Social Justice Becomes a Supreme Court Justice

RICHARD MICHELSON

ILLUSTRATED BY STACY INNERST

CALKINS CREEK
AN IMPRINT OF ASTRA BOOKS FOR YOUNG READERS
New York

Louis Brandeis is only five years old, but he knows his parents came to America in 1848, eight years before he was born.

His mother, Frederika, says Prague was often dangerous for Jews attending school or the theater.

"Any fool knows that everyone should be treated equally regardless of their religion," his father, Adolph, adds.

Louis knows his family is Jewish even though they don't belong to a synagogue. And on Christmas, they have a tree and exchange presents.

His mother says that sharing food and helping those less fortunate is the best way to be nearer to God. She says religious rituals are less important than being a kind person.

Uncle Lewis Dembitz is a lawyer who likes to debate with his sister, Louis's mother. He says Jews can be kind AND follow their Orthodox traditions, too. At his house, Louis eats kosher meals, and welcomes the Sabbath on Friday evenings.

The Civil War is being fought near his home in Louisville, Kentucky. Louis can hear gunfire. Sometimes he helps his mother carry food and coffee to the Union soldiers who are fighting to help free the enslaved.

His mother says that one person should never be allowed to own another person.

"Any fool knows that all people should be treated equally regardless of their race," his father adds.

Sitting around the dinner table with his older sisters, Fannie and Amy, and his big brother Alfred, Louis loves to listen as his family discusses politics and art and music and the books they're reading.

He can't wait to start school and learn to read and write and to recite poems.

Louis loves studying science and math and history. Sometimes he makes foolish errors on his homework, but his teachers give him articles written by experts so he can learn from his mistakes.

At sixteen Louis receives a special gold medal from the University of the Public Schools in Louisville for "pre-eminence in all his studies." His knees tremble when he thinks about speaking in front of the whole school.

On graduation day, he feels lucky to wake up with laryngitis.

Louis loves learning but he always finds time to play. "Any fool knows that leisure is as important as a school education," his father says, encouraging his children to hike and swim.

"Any fool knows that friends and music and bathing in a river are more important than money and property," his father adds.

The Civil War has ended. The Brandeis grain business prospered selling food to the Union army, but Louis's family is now moving back to Europe until America's economy improves.

The principal at Louis's German school doesn't believe a poor American student can keep up with the class. He tells Louis to come back with his birth certificate and take an exam.

"The fact that I am here is proof of my birth,"
Louis insists. He argues that everyone deserves
an equal chance to prove themselves. He promises
to leave the school if he doesn't measure up. Louis
doesn't stop talking until the principal agrees.

He has argued his first case. And won!

By the end of the year Louis has the highest marks in his class, but he is homesick. He is happy when his father decides to move the family back to America.

Louis is eighteen years old. He has seen how some people are treated poorly because of their race or their religion or because they are poor. *If I were a lawyer like Uncle Dembitz,* he thinks, *I could fight for those who need extra help.*

Although he has never been to college, Louis borrows the tuition money and applies to Harvard Law School.

Louis's knees tremble as he enters the admissions office. The dean explains that Louis would be the youngest student and the only Jew in his class. But Louis argues that everyone deserves a chance to prove themselves.

Another win!

Studying by the gas lamp's flickering light weakens Louis's eye muscles. A doctor tells him to find a career where he doesn't have to read so much. Louis convinces his best friend, Samuel Warren, to recite the textbooks to him.

Louis has the highest grade average in Harvard's history, and he wins the class prize. But the dean explains that Harvard rules state that you must be twenty-one years old to graduate. Louis is only twenty. Louis knows that isn't fair. He argues his case until Harvard agrees to change the rule.

Louis is now a lawyer with lots of wealthy clients. They hire Louis when they need help, but they think they are superior to him because he is Jewish.

Even Samuel Warren's fiancée refuses to invite Louis to their wedding. But when a high-society newspaper takes secret unflattering photographs of her, she asks her new husband to enlist Louis's help to stop them from being published.

Louis longs for the day when he can spend his time fighting for the poor and the needy. But for now, he has bills to pay.

Louis writes an article arguing that everyone has the right to their own privacy. It is so popular that Louis loses his own privacy. His picture is in all the Boston newspapers.

The Boston Daily Globe. FINAL

Louis's law firm is busier than ever. But he still leaves the office every day at five o'clock to fish and hike and spend time with his wife and two daughters.

He encourages his staff to do the same. "Any fool knows that if you work twelve hours a day, you get less than eight hours of work done, because your mind becomes too tired to think," he tells them.

America is also busier than ever. Industries are booming!

It seems like everyone is moving to the city looking for a job. Factory owners are getting wealthy by paying low wages and forcing their employees to work from early morning until late at night. Some mothers barely get to see their children.

When a group of women ask him to help them fight for shorter working hours, Louis takes the case for free. "Any fool knows that helping to change unfair laws is more important than money," he tells them.

With help from his sister-in-law, Louis gathers over one hundred pages of articles and expert opinions to prove that long hours are dangerous to women's health and safety. His teachers have taught him well.

Louis knows men should also spend more time at home, but he'll worry about that later.

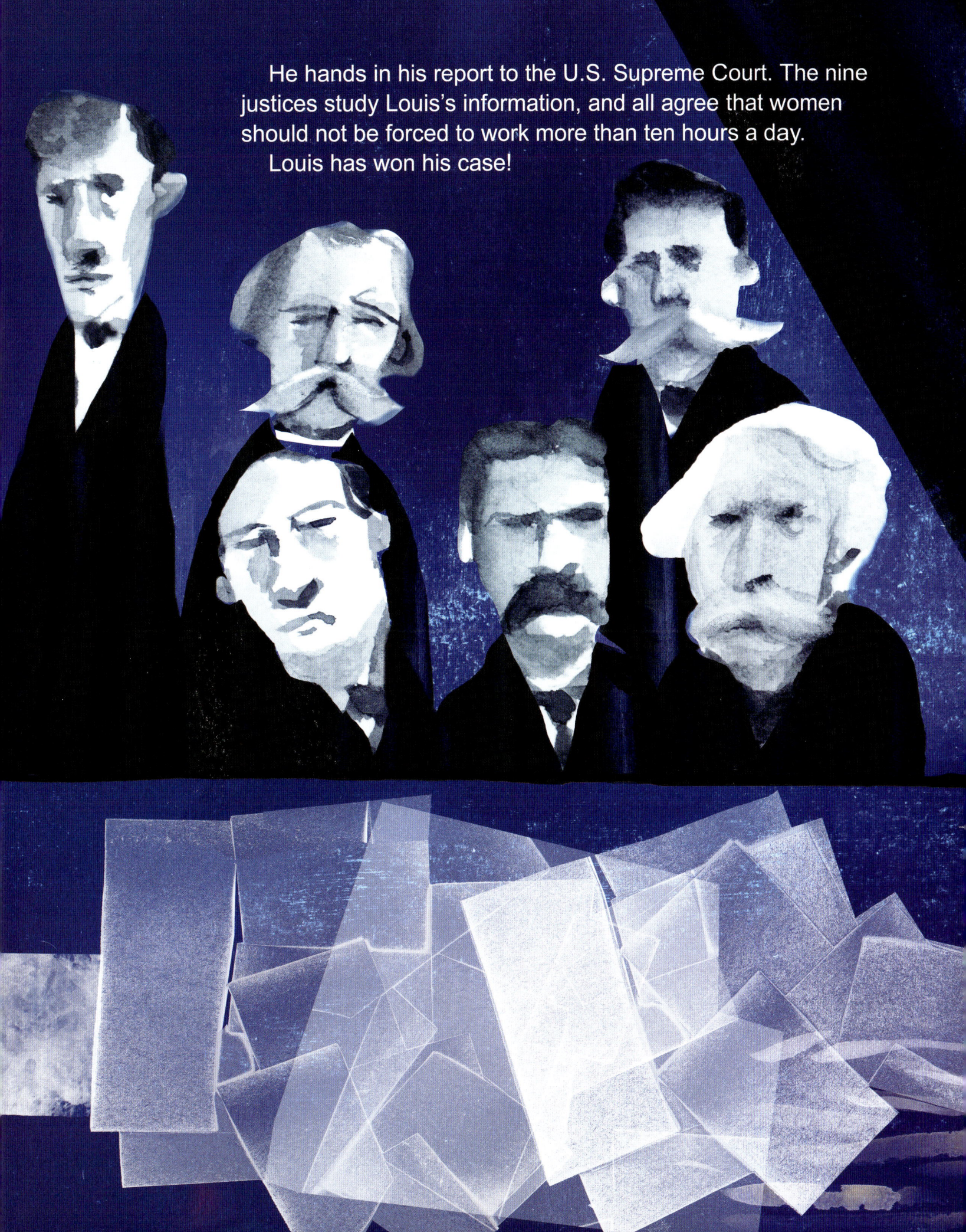

He hands in his report to the U.S. Supreme Court. The nine justices study Louis's information, and all agree that women should not be forced to work more than ten hours a day. Louis has won his case!

Soon, other lawyers start gathering facts to support their legal arguments. They call their documents "Brandeis Briefs" in honor of Louis. But Louis calls it common sense, or "what any fool knows."

Louis is happy to be known as a "crusader for social justice."
He exposes insurance companies that cheat workers. He
unmasks railroad tycoons who overcharge customers. Louis
attacks using legal arguments and facts. He isn't afraid of
anyone. He even accuses the president of the United States of
not honoring his promise to save America's forests. Louis doesn't
give up until President Taft protects public lands so all citizens
can hike, fish, and swim.

Louis is now one of the most famous lawyers in America.

America is growing faster than ever.
Every month thousands of Jews are
forced to leave Russia and eastern Europe.
Many refugees agree with a group called
Zionists, who believe that Jews should have
their own country, where they will always be
treated equally. But for now, they enter the
United States seeking safety and the
freedom to practice their religion.

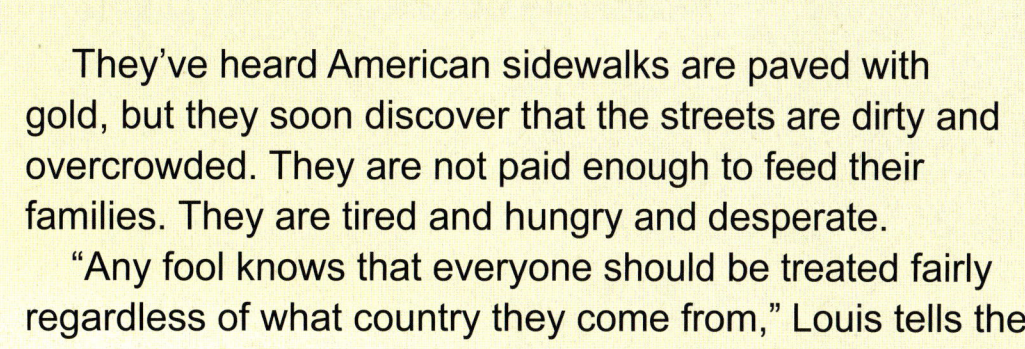

They've heard American sidewalks are paved with gold, but they soon discover that the streets are dirty and overcrowded. They are not paid enough to feed their families. They are tired and hungry and desperate.

"Any fool knows that everyone should be treated fairly regardless of what country they come from," Louis tells the sixty thousand garment workers, mostly Jewish men, who have joined together and refused to work until factory conditions improve.

Louis gathers articles and expert opinions to prove that happier employees work harder and make their companies more money. He convinces their bosses to raise wages and shorten hours.

The newly elected president, Woodrow Wilson, admires Louis's ideas about fairness. He knows Louis can help him fight against dishonest business and government officials who take advantage of the public they pretend to serve. He nominates Louis to serve on the Supreme Court.

Louis is called a radical, a socialist, a muckraker, and a traitor.

Louis listens to all the bad things his enemies are saying about him. It looks like the Senate will not accept the president's recommendation. But Louis knows he has fought for ordinary citizens over the years and is known as "the people's attorney." He asks for their help.

Senators start receiving letters from clergy, lawyers, teachers, social workers, students, and laborers.

On June 1, 1916, the Senate votes: 47 members in favor and 22 against.

Four days later, Louis Brandeis is sworn in as the first Jewish justice on the Supreme Court.

Louis knows for certain that his fight for social justice has just begun.

Louis Brandeis, around 1910

More About the Supreme Court

Louis Brandeis, the son of immigrants, was the first American Jew to sit on the Supreme Court. From 1789—when the court was first established—until 1916 (when Brandeis was appointed), all sixty-six justices had been white, male, and Christian.

The first Black justice, Thurgood Marshall, was not appointed until 1967. The first female justice, Sandra Day O'Connor, wasn't appointed until 1981, and the first Latina, Sonia Sotomayor, not until 2009. In 2022, Ketanji Brown Jackson became the first Black woman to be seated on the bench. While the court is becoming more diverse, there has still never been an Asian American, Pacific Islander, or Native American appointed.

The president nominates the justice, who must then be confirmed by the Senate. The Supreme Court's job is to settle arguments when people disagree. The justices must make their decisions based on their understanding of the rules of the country as written down in the United States Constitution.

Louis Brandeis and the Right to Privacy

Although there are different theories as to the origins of Louis's famous article "The Right to Privacy," one popular opinion is that it came about at the request of his best friend and business partner, Samuel Warren, whose socialite wife, Mabel Bayard Warren, complained about her unflattering appearances in the newspaper gossip columns. Mabel had refused to allow Louis to attend her wedding, because she believed Jews were inferior to Christians. But her antisemitic views did not stop her from urging her husband to enlist Louis's help in writing the article, nor did it stop Louis from arguing her case and stating his beliefs.

The "right to privacy" was one of the most groundbreaking ideas in American legal history. The thought that someone could "invade your privacy" did not exist prior to Louis's article. As a Supreme Court judge, Louis would protest against allowing police to try to catch criminals by eavesdropping on private telephone conversations. He warned that "the progress of science in furnishing the Government with means of espionage is not likely to stop with wiretapping."

Louis understood that many celebrities have invited attention. Today, social media encourages all of us to share our every picture and thought. But Louis was a very private person and believed that "the right most valued . . . is the right to be let alone."

Louis Brandeis and Women's Rights

Louis agreed to help the National Consumers League fight to shorten working hours for women. He won his case, but also relied on society's prejudices that men were stronger than women. Among the experts he quoted was a male doctor who reported, incorrectly, that "women's blood had more water than men's blood," and women were, therefore, weaker. Louis also explained that men could rest after their workday ended, but "for the working-girl on her return from the factory . . . she should be learning to keep house."

It is hard to know how much of this was a legal strategy and how much Louis believed. We do know Louis originally opposed voting rights for women but he learned from his mistakes. He wrote, "the insight women have shown into problems that men do not understand has convinced me that women should have the ballot." Louis became a strong supporter of women's suffrage.

Louis Brandeis and the "Public Good"

Louis lived modestly—though he sometimes splurged on ice cream. "Some men . . . delight in automobiles and yachts," he wrote to his brother, "but my luxury is . . . the pleasure of taking up a problem and solving it for the people without receiving compensation."

Louis had made more than a million dollars in his law firm when he decided he would not turn away anyone seeking social justice who could not afford his fee. Soon most of his work involved championing causes to benefit society and help the poor. That is why he became known as a "crusader for social justice," and "the people's lawyer."

Other lawyers thought he was crazy to work for free, but today, thanks to Louis, many law firms include some "pro bono" (which means "for the public good" in Latin) work in their practices.

Louis Brandeis and Savings Bank Life Insurance

Working men would often pay small amounts of money every month to life insurance companies in exchange for a promise that the company would help their wives and children buy food and pay rent if the worker died. But Louis discovered that in eight out of every ten cases, the company would find a reason to cancel the policy before they had to pay their share.

Louis convinced banks that they could sell insurance at lower costs, pay what they promised, and still be profitable. He called Savings Bank Life Insurance one of his greatest achievements.

Louis Brandeis and Monopolies

If you have ever played the board game Monopoly, the aim is for one person to own everything, and all other players to end up penniless. The creators of the game, originally called The Landlord's Game, wanted to teach people the dangers of a winner-take-all system.

Louis wanted everyone to be a winner. He thought that wealth should be shared by all the workers. Louis argued that "we may have democracy, or we may have wealth concentrated in the hands of a few, but we can't have both."

Louis Brandeis, J. P. Morgan, and the Railroads

A man named J. P. Morgan was one of America's most powerful tycoons. He wanted to own all the New England railroads. Instead of paying his workers enough, or charging fair prices, Morgan "donated" to politicians so they would give him special favors.

Louis worked without pay to prove that Morgan was dishonest, but Morgan paid newspapers to print articles attacking Louis. Finally, after nine years, Louis won his case, which helped to break up the railroad monopoly. Louis later wrote a book called *Other People's Money and How Bankers Use It* in which he tried to expose the system that

allowed "lying and sneaking" people like Morgan to become wealthy, while keeping most honest, hardworking people poor.

Louis Brandeis, President William Howard Taft, and Land Conservation

President William Howard Taft promised to protect public lands for recreation. Instead, he allowed his secretary of the interior to sell mining rights. Louis discovered that President Taft had lied about the facts of the case. At that time, most people trusted the government and thought it was "ungentlemanly" and "rude" to accuse a president of lying. But Louis said that "the only title in our democracy superior to that of President is the title of citizen." He wrote that "people with power should use it for the benefit of everyone without power," and that "if the government becomes the lawbreaker, it breeds contempt for law." This saved the Alaskan forests, and Louis became a hero to the conservation movement.

Louis Brandeis and Labor Unions

As industry grew and people crowded into cities, many business owners insisted on low wages and long hours that affected workers' health and safety. Eventually, employees banded together in groups called unions, which could threaten to strike (stop work and make the factories shut down). Louis was most often on the side of the unions, but he also knew that business owners needed to make a profit.

When the New York garment workers went on strike, both the strikers and factory owners trusted Louis to help find a solution. Louis persuaded the bosses that if they paid higher wages, and gave more time off, they would have more productive workers, and everyone would make more money. Everyone, that is, except Louis, who refused payment.

Louis Brandeis and Zionism

Louis was not religious, nor did he follow Orthodox traditions like his Uncle Dembitz. But that doesn't mean he didn't experience antisemitism. In the years leading up to World War I, attacks on Jews were growing. The Zionists wanted to create a Jewish homeland where everyone would work together for the common good, sharing the natural resources and the food they grew. They believed in free public education and equality for all. Louis envisioned a Jewish homeland that gave equal political rights and economic opportunity to its Arab citizens.

When Louis joined the Zionists, they were a small ragtag group of dreamers supported by few American Jews. Most immigrants wanted to be thought of as 100 percent American and worried they would be accused of loyalty to a Jewish state rather than the United States. But many Jews looked up to Louis as a modern-day prophet, and under Louis's leadership, Zionism became "fashionable" and a major

political movement. As the Nazi Party gathered power in Germany toward the end of Louis's life, it turned out, sadly, that Louis was correct; Jews did need a safe place to live, even if the reality of Israel could not live up to Louis's idealistic vision.

Brandeis in the early 1900s

Brandeis as a toddler with his mother Frederika

Brandeis at age 8

Timeline

1856   Louis David Brandeis is born November 13.

1873   Louis attends Annen-Realschule, a school in Dresden, Germany.

1875   Louis enters Harvard Law School. He changes his middle name to Dembitz in honor of his uncle.

1879   Warren & Brandeis law firm opens for business.

1890   Louis writes an article for the *Harvard Law Review*, titled "The Right to Privacy." Although the article is credited to both Louis Brandeis and Samuel Warren, Warren suggested it, but Louis wrote most of it.

1891   Louis marries Alice Goldmark, and they have two daughters: Susan, born in 1893, and Elizabeth, born in 1896.

1905–1907   Louis fights corruption by insurance companies and, thanks to his influence, Massachusetts Savings Bank Life Insurance program is signed into law.

1907–1913   Louis fights to prevent J. P. Morgan's railroad monopoly.

1908   Louis argues *Muller v. Oregon* in the U. S. Supreme Court and wins his case to limit women's working hours by presenting his "Brandeis Brief."

1910   Louis accuses President William Howard Taft and his secretary of the interior, Richard Ballinger, of dishonesty. He protects Alaskan Conservation Land.

1910 Louis negotiates to end the New York City garment workers' strike.

1914–1916 Louis becomes chairman of the Executive Committee of Zionist Affairs. He resigns from his position when he is appointed to the Supreme Court, though he remains involved with the group and in 1920 is made honorary president of the World Zionist Organization.

1916 President Woodrow Wilson nominates Louis to the Supreme Court, and he is confirmed as the first Jewish justice.

1939 Louis retires from the Court on February 13.

1941 Louis dies on Sunday, October 5, at his home in Washington, DC. He is eighty-four years old.

Alice Brandeis (née Goldmark), Louis's wife

Brandeis at age 38

The Legacy of Louis Brandeis

Louis Brandeis dedicated his life to helping those less fortunate. He believed that every person deserved dignity, leisure, and privacy regardless of their race, religion, or wealth. Many lawyers try to use the law to keep order; Louis used it to create change.

Due to his influence, fair wages, limited working hours, social security, unemployment insurance, health and safety regulations, and the right of employees to organize are now all protected by law.

Many of Louis's opinions are more important today than ever; immigrants are again being unfairly blamed for America's problems, the richest 1 percent of our citizens hold more wealth than the bottom 40 percent, social media companies spy on us in our houses and sell our most personal information for profit, and climate-change skeptics refuse to accept scientific data, putting our planet in danger. It is easy to lose hope.

But Louis was an optimist. He trusted people to find the truth when given the correct facts and expert opinions. Throughout his life, he continued to put his faith in education and common sense.

May we all follow his lead and learn from our mistakes. May we, like Louis Brandeis, leave the world a better place than we found it.

The US Supreme Court, 1924. Bottom row (left to right): Willis Van Devanter, Joseph McKenna, William Howard Taft, Oliver Wendell Holmes Jr., James Clark McReynolds. Top row (left to right): Pierce Butler, Louis Brandeis, George Sutherland, Edward Sanford.

Bibliography

Quotes attributed to Louis Brandeis are taken from his speeches and letters, although some phrases are shortened and rearranged for precision and rhythm. Adolph Brandeis's dialogue is loosely translated and paraphrased by the author, but the meaning and tone are taken from his letters and Louis's reminiscences.

Brandeis, Louis D. *Letters of Louis D. Brandeis*. Edited by Melvin I. Urofsky and David W. Levy. 5 vols. Albany: SUNY Press, 1971.

———. *Mr. Justice Brandeis: Essays*. New Haven, CT: Yale University Press, 1932.

———. *The Social and Economic Views of Mr. Justice Brandeis*. New York: Vanguard, 1930.

Dalin, David D. *Jewish Justices of the Supreme Court: From Brandeis to Kagan*. Waltham, MA: Brandeis University Press, 2017.

Freedman, Suzanne. *Louis Brandeis: The People's Justice*. New York: Enslow Publishing, 1996.

Lief, Alfred. *Brandeis: The Personal History of an American Ideal*. New York: Stackpole Sons, 1936.

Rosen, Jeffrey. *Louis D. Brandeis: American Prophet*. New Haven, CT: Yale University Press, 2016.

Strum, Philippa. *Louis D. Brandeis: Justice for the People*. Cambridge, MA: Harvard University Press, 1984.

Urofsky, Melvin I. *Louis D. Brandeis: A Life*. New York: Pantheon, 2019.

Acknowledgments

In memory of social justice warriors: attorney Philip Coltman, attorney David Schechter, and Judge Eli Mellan.

With thanks to David Dalin, Jonathan Sarna, Melvin Urofsky, and Rabbi Howard Voss-Altman for their scholarship, and Sue Berger Ramin, director of Brandeis University Press, for her encouragement.

Picture Credits

For Jennifer, who taught me "that friends and music and bathing in a river are more important than money and property" —*RM*

For Gladis —*SI*

For information about permission to reproduce selections from this book, please contact permissions@astrapublishinghouse.com.

ISBN: 978-1-6626-8063-2 (hc)
ISBN: 978-1-6626-8064-9 (eBook)
Library of Congress Control Number: 2024947356

First edition
10 9 8 7 6 5 4 3 2 1

Design by Barbara Grzeslo
The text is set in Arial.
The illustrations are done in gouache, acrylic, colored pencil, and digital.